I LOVE YOU FOR YOUR *PERSONALITY* BUT THAT IS A REALLY NICE BONUS!

> "keep taking chances - make life your bitch and never give up!"

Date: /   /

THINGS TO BE GRATEFUL FOR TODAY

*"Have dreams and dream big!
Dream without fear"*

Date: /   /

THINGS TO BE GRATEFUL FOR TODAY

"Believe in miracles but above all believe in yourself!"
And never forget I Fucking Love You!

Date: /   /

THINGS TO BE GRATEFUL FOR TODAY

"Let your dreams be as big as your desire to succeed"

Date: /   /

THINGS TO BE GRATEFUL FOR TODAY

> *"Never downgrade your dreams, reach for the stars and believe in your self power"*

Date: /   /

THINGS TO BE GRATEFUL FOR TODAY

> *"They say I dream too big. I say they think too small"* - Unknown

Date: /   /

THINGS TO BE GRATEFUL FOR TODAY

> *"Never be afraid to start something new, if you fail it is just temporary, if you believe and persist you will succeed"*

Date: /   /

THINGS TO BE GRATEFUL FOR TODAY

> *"Your driving force and your power lies within you and the size of your dreams, never give up!"*

Date: /   /

THINGS TO BE GRATEFUL FOR TODAY

> *"Wherever you go, go with all your heart."*
> *- Confucius*

Date: /   /

THINGS TO BE GRATEFUL FOR TODAY

> *"Build your own dreams or you will end up building someone else's dreams"*

Date: /   /

THINGS TO BE GRATEFUL FOR TODAY

> *"Your dreams and your goals are the seeds of your own success"*

Date: /   /

THINGS TO BE GRATEFUL FOR TODAY

"Never give up, keep going no matter what!"

Date: /   /

THINGS TO BE GRATEFUL FOR TODAY

"Start where you are and take chances"

Date: /   /

THINGS TO BE GRATEFUL FOR TODAY

> *"If you never give up you become unbeatable, just keep going!"*

Date: /   /

THINGS TO BE GRATEFUL FOR TODAY

"Life isn't about finding yourself. Life is about creating yourself." - George Bernard Shaw

Date: /   /

THINGS TO BE GRATEFUL FOR TODAY

> "Change your life today. Don't gamble on the future, act now, without delay." — Simone de Beauvoir

Date: /   /

THINGS TO BE GRATEFUL FOR TODAY

"Keep your motivation and your momentum with a new goal every day!"

Date: /   /

THINGS TO BE GRATEFUL FOR TODAY

"Aim for the stars to keep your dreams alive"

Date: /   /

THINGS TO BE GRATEFUL FOR TODAY

"When life gives you lemons, add a little gin and tonic"

Date: /   /

THINGS TO BE GRATEFUL FOR TODAY

> *"There are no limits to what you can achieve if you believe in your dreams"*

Date: /   /

THINGS TO BE GRATEFUL FOR TODAY

> "When you feel you are defeated, just remember, you have the power to move on, it is all in your mind"

Date: /   /

THINGS TO BE GRATEFUL FOR TODAY

"Don't just dream your dreams, make them happen!"

Date: /   /

THINGS TO BE GRATEFUL FOR TODAY

"Opportunity comes to those who never give up"

Date: /   /

THINGS TO BE GRATEFUL FOR TODAY

"You are the creator of your own opportunities"

Date: /   /

THINGS TO BE GRATEFUL FOR TODAY

> *"Always aim for bigger goals, they have the power to keep you motivated"*

Date: /   /

THINGS TO BE GRATEFUL FOR TODAY

> *"Success is not a place or a destination, it is a way of thinking while always having a new goal in mind"*

Date: /   /

THINGS TO BE GRATEFUL FOR TODAY

"Every achievement starts with a dream and a goal in mind"

Date: /   /

THINGS TO BE GRATEFUL FOR TODAY

> *"Change the world one dream at a time, believe in your dreams"*

Date: /   /

THINGS TO BE GRATEFUL FOR TODAY

> *"Never loose confidence in your dreams, there will be obstacles and defeats, but you will always win if you persist"*

Date: /   /

THINGS TO BE GRATEFUL FOR TODAY

> *""Never wait for someone else to validate your existence, you are the creator of your own destiny"*

Date: /   /

THINGS TO BE GRATEFUL FOR TODAY

> *"Dreams are the energy that power your life"*

Date: /   /

THINGS TO BE GRATEFUL FOR TODAY

> "Dreams make things happen, nothing is impossible as long as you believe." - Anonymous

Date: /   /

THINGS TO BE GRATEFUL FOR TODAY

"Always dream big and follow your heart"

Date: /   /

THINGS TO BE GRATEFUL FOR TODAY

"Never stop dreaming." - Anonymous

Date: /   /

THINGS TO BE GRATEFUL FOR TODAY

> *"Everything you dream is possible as long as you believe in yourself"*

Date: /   /

THINGS TO BE GRATEFUL FOR TODAY

"Dream big, it's the first step to success" - Anonymous

Date: /   /

THINGS TO BE GRATEFUL FOR TODAY

> *"A successful person is someone that understands temporary defeat as a learning process, never give up!"*

Date: /   /

THINGS TO BE GRATEFUL FOR TODAY

> *"Motivation comes from working on our dreams and from taking action to achieve our goals"*

Date: /   /

THINGS TO BE GRATEFUL FOR TODAY

> *"Dreams are the foundation to our imagination and success"*

Date: /   /

THINGS TO BE GRATEFUL FOR TODAY

> *"Your mission in life should be to thrive and not merely survive"*

Date: /   /

THINGS TO BE GRATEFUL FOR TODAY

> *"Doing what you believe in, and going after your dreams will only result in success."* - Anonymous

Date: /   /

THINGS TO BE GRATEFUL FOR TODAY

"The right time to start something new is now"

Date: /   /

THINGS TO BE GRATEFUL FOR TODAY

> *"Be brave, fight for what you believe in and make your dreams a reality."* - Anonymous

Date: /   /

THINGS TO BE GRATEFUL FOR TODAY

> *"Put more energy into your dreams than Into your fears and you will see positive results"*

Date: /   /

THINGS TO BE GRATEFUL FOR TODAY

"Let your dreams be bigger than your fears and your actions louder than your words." - Anonymous

Date: /   /

THINGS TO BE GRATEFUL FOR TODAY

> *"Always keep moving forward to keep your balance, if you stop dreaming you will fall"*

Date: /   /

THINGS TO BE GRATEFUL FOR TODAY

> *"Start every day with a goal in mind and make it happen with your actions"*

Date: /   /

THINGS TO BE GRATEFUL FOR TODAY

"Dream. Believe. Create. Succeed" - Anonymous

Date: /   /

THINGS TO BE GRATEFUL FOR TODAY

> *"You are never to old to set new goals and achieve them, keep on dreaming!"*

Date: /   /

THINGS TO BE GRATEFUL FOR TODAY

> *"If you have big dreams you will always have big reasons to wake up every day"*

Date: /   /

THINGS TO BE GRATEFUL FOR TODAY

> *"Difficulties are nothing more than opportunities in disguise, keep on trying and you will succeed"*

Date: /   /

THINGS TO BE GRATEFUL FOR TODAY

> *"To achieve our dreams we must first overcome our fear of failure"*

Date: /   /

THINGS TO BE GRATEFUL FOR TODAY

> *"Always have a powerful reason to wake up every new morning, set goals and follow your dreams"*

Date: /   /

THINGS TO BE GRATEFUL FOR TODAY

"Use failure as a motivation tool not as a sign of defeat"

Date: /   /

THINGS TO BE GRATEFUL FOR TODAY

> *"Never let your dreams die for fear of failure, defeat is just temporary; your dreams are your power"*

Date: /   /

THINGS TO BE GRATEFUL FOR TODAY

> "A failure is a lesson, not a loss. It is a temporary and sometimes necessary detour, not a dead end"

Date: /   /

THINGS TO BE GRATEFUL FOR TODAY

"Have faith in the future but above all in yourself"

Date: /   /

THINGS TO BE GRATEFUL FOR TODAY

"Those who live in the past limit their future"
- Anonymous

Date: /   /

THINGS TO BE GRATEFUL FOR TODAY

> *"Your future is created by what you do today not tomorrow"* - Anonymous

Date: /   /

THINGS TO BE GRATEFUL FOR TODAY

"Never let your doubt blind your goals, for your future lies in your ability, not your failure" — Anonymous

Date: /   /

THINGS TO BE GRATEFUL FOR TODAY

*"Don't go into something to test the waters,
go into things to make waves"* — Anonymous

Date: /   /

THINGS TO BE GRATEFUL FOR TODAY

"Laughter is the shock absorber that softens and minimizes the bumps of life" — Anonymous

Date: /   /

THINGS TO BE GRATEFUL FOR TODAY

"Dream – Believe – Achieve"

Date: /   /

THINGS TO BE GRATEFUL FOR TODAY

"Make your own destiny. Don't wait for it to come to you, life is not a rehearsal" — *Anonymous*

Date: /   /

THINGS TO BE GRATEFUL FOR TODAY

"If you want to feel rich, just count all the things you have that money can't buy" — *Anonymous*

Date: /   /

THINGS TO BE GRATEFUL FOR TODAY

> *"Never give up on a dream just because of the time it will take to accomplish it. The time will pass anyway."* — Anonymous

Date: /   /

THINGS TO BE GRATEFUL FOR TODAY

> "I am never a failure until I begin blaming others"
> - Anonymous

Date: /   /

THINGS TO BE GRATEFUL FOR TODAY

"Your only limitation is your imagination" — *Anonymous*

Date: /   /

THINGS TO BE GRATEFUL FOR TODAY

"Some pursue success and happiness – others create it" — Anonymous

Date: /   /

THINGS TO BE GRATEFUL FOR TODAY

> *"Anything worth doing is worth doing well"*
> — Anonymous

Date: /   /

THINGS TO BE GRATEFUL FOR TODAY

> *"It's better to have an impossible dream than no dream at all."* – Anonymous

Date: /   /

THINGS TO BE GRATEFUL FOR TODAY

"Never let defeat have the last word" — Anonymous

Date: /   /

THINGS TO BE GRATEFUL FOR TODAY

> *"The winner always has a plan; The loser always has an excuse"* — *Anonymous*

Date: /   /

THINGS TO BE GRATEFUL FOR TODAY

> *"There is no elevator to success.
> You have to take the stairs"* — Anonymous

Date: /   /

THINGS TO BE GRATEFUL FOR TODAY

"Don't let yesterday's disappointments, overshadow tomorrow's achievements" — Anonymous

Date: /   /

THINGS TO BE GRATEFUL FOR TODAY

"We are limited, not by our abilities, but by our vision"
— Anonymous

Date: /   /

THINGS TO BE GRATEFUL FOR TODAY

"Dreams don't come true. Dreams are true"
— Anonymous

Date: /   /

THINGS TO BE GRATEFUL FOR TODAY

> "Happiness is not something you get, but something you do" — Anonymous

Date: /   /

THINGS TO BE GRATEFUL FOR TODAY

> *"A journey of a thousand miles must begin with a single step."* — *Lao Tzu*

Date: /   /

THINGS TO BE GRATEFUL FOR TODAY

"Try and fail, but don't fail to try" — Anonymous

Date: /   /

THINGS TO BE GRATEFUL FOR TODAY

"You risk more when you don't take any risks"

Date: /   /

THINGS TO BE GRATEFUL FOR TODAY

> *"A diamond is a chunk of coal that made good under pressure"* — Anonymous

Date: /   /

THINGS TO BE GRATEFUL FOR TODAY

> *"No dreamer is ever too small; no dream is ever too big."* – Anonymous

Date: /   /

THINGS TO BE GRATEFUL FOR TODAY

"All our tomorrows depend on today" — *Anonymous*

Date: /   /

THINGS TO BE GRATEFUL FOR TODAY

> *"Remember yesterday, dream of tomorrow, but live for today"* — Anonymous

Date: /   /

THINGS TO BE GRATEFUL FOR TODAY

> "Dream is not what you see in sleep, dream is the thing which does not let you sleep" — Anonymous

Date: /   /

THINGS TO BE GRATEFUL FOR TODAY

> *"Don't be pushed by your problems.
> Be led by your dreams"* — Anonymous

Date: /   /

THINGS TO BE GRATEFUL FOR TODAY

> "Dreams give purpose to your life and meaning to your existence"

Date: /   /

THINGS TO BE GRATEFUL FOR TODAY

> *"Once you have a dream put all your heart and soul to achieve it"*

Date: /   /

THINGS TO BE GRATEFUL FOR TODAY

"Follow your heart and your dreams will come true"
— Anonymous

Date: /   /

THINGS TO BE GRATEFUL FOR TODAY

> *"You create your life by following your dreams with decisive actions"*

Date: /   /

THINGS TO BE GRATEFUL FOR TODAY

> *"Without dreams you lose interest in life, you have no energy to move forward"*

Date: /   /

THINGS TO BE GRATEFUL FOR TODAY

"Difficult roads often lead to beautiful destinations"

Date: /   /

THINGS TO BE GRATEFUL FOR TODAY

> *"The road to success is always full of surprises and temporary failures, real success comes to those who persist"*

Date: /   /

THINGS TO BE GRATEFUL FOR TODAY

"Believe in yourself and you will be unstoppable"

Date: /   /

THINGS TO BE GRATEFUL FOR TODAY

"Today is another chance to get better"

Date: /   /

THINGS TO BE GRATEFUL FOR TODAY

"To live a creative life, we must lose our fear of being wrong" - Anonymous

Date: /   /

THINGS TO BE GRATEFUL FOR TODAY

> *"Make each day count, you will never have this day again"*

Date: /   /

THINGS TO BE GRATEFUL FOR TODAY

> *"If you do what you always did,
> you will get what you always got"* - Anonymous

Date: /   /

THINGS TO BE GRATEFUL FOR TODAY

> *"It's not what you look at that matters, it's what you see"* - Anonymous

Date: /   /

THINGS TO BE GRATEFUL FOR TODAY

"You are capable of amazing things"

Date: /   /

THINGS TO BE GRATEFUL FOR TODAY

"Believe in yourself and you will be unstoppable"

Date: /   /

THINGS TO BE GRATEFUL FOR TODAY

> *"Successful people make a habit of doing what unsuccessful people don't want to do"*
> *— Anonymous*

Date: /   /

THINGS TO BE GRATEFUL FOR TODAY

> *"To be the best you must be able to handle the worst"* - Anonymous

Date: /   /

THINGS TO BE GRATEFUL FOR TODAY

"Nothing worth having comes easy" - Anonymous

Date: /   /

THINGS TO BE GRATEFUL FOR TODAY

"Follow your dreams, they know the way"

Date: /   /

THINGS TO BE GRATEFUL FOR TODAY

"I Fucking Love You!"

Date: /   /

THINGS TO BE GRATEFUL FOR TODAY

We hope you enjoyed your journal – notebook, please let us know if you liked it by writing a review, it means a lot to us.

Thank you!

DESIGNED BY Sweary Press Gifts FOR:

CREATIVE JOURNALS FACTORY

FIND OTHER BEAUTIFUL JOURNALS, DIARIES AND NOTEBOOKS AT:

www.CreativeJournalsFactory.com

JOURNALS - DIARIES - NOTEBOOKS - COLORING BOOKS

CPSIA information can be obtained
at www.ICGtesting.com
Printed in the USA
BVHW020219170423
662475BV00009B/204